The 'How To' Book for Solving Difficult Sudoku Puzzles

An illustrated methodology
For quickly solving difficult and complex
Sudoku puzzles

		8					3	
4	5			1		2		
			8	3	5			
		5					8	2
			5		2			
7	6					9		
			1	7	6			
		1		5			2	6
	9					5		

Sudoku puzzles © Wayne Gould

A step-by-step tutorial
Written by Charles Brownell
Justine Brownell, Editor

Dedication

This book is dedicated to all the Sudoku players who have worked diligently on a puzzle only to get part way through and find it couldn't be completed without guessing. How frustrating! Guessing shouldn't be part of a game of logic. I hope this book will provide you with a way to eliminate your frustration and help you solve all your Sudoku puzzles quickly and easily.

Table of Contents

Introduction

This book is for everyone, from beginners to expert Sudoku players. If you are a beginner and don't know what Sudoku is or how to play I refer you to the following website. http://www.sudoku.com/howtoplay.html *

My first thought is, do you need to read this book? Please try to solve the puzzle on the first page. If you got it in less than 15 minutes then you probably don't need to read this book. If not, you'll get something out of reading it.

I use the standard 9x9 grid, not the 5x5 or any other variation of the game. Perhaps the methods discussed here may apply to those versions as well.

When I first tried Sudoku I spent hours racking my brain over the simplest puzzles. I thought there had to be a better way. I did an Internet search and found a few tutorials that provided some guidance but not a definitive methodology for solving puzzles.

My goal is to solve the puzzles **quickly**. I love the game. I don't mind spending a few minutes here and there, but I don't want to spend hours working a puzzle.

Over a period of about a year I devised a methodology that works well for me and I share it here with you now. Personally I learn best by doing, so I will walk you through solving two 'difficult' puzzles.

Have you ever had a puzzle that you can't solve using the standard rules of elimination? You get to a certain point and there doesn't seem to be a solution. This methodology will help you solve those puzzles.

*Sudoku.com is owned and operated by RealNetworks, Inc.

Definitions

So that we have a common vocabulary I'll define a few of the terms I use.

Rows run from left to right and columns from top to bottom. I label individual squares where you write the numbers as 'squares' and the groups of nine squares I call 'Boxes'. I number the Boxes as follows:

	1			2			3	
	4			5			6	
	7			8			9	

A final word before we begin. I know it will take an hour or two to go through this book and learn the methodology, but you will be rewarded with quick solutions to difficult puzzles in the end. Hang in there. You may be tempted to simply read through the book, but I believe you'll get more out of it if you work through the puzzles on your own paper.

Puzzle #1

To begin you'll need an 8.5" x 11" piece of paper with a Sudoku grid. I like to use a large sheet of paper because I write a lot of numbers in the individual squares. I like to use a spreadsheet to create the grid because I can have bold lines between the Boxes just like the published Sudoku puzzles.

Here's your first puzzle. It is rated as difficult. Did you try and solve it? If not, give it a try now. Did you finish in less than 15 minutes? If so, please go to puzzle #2.

		8					3	
4	5			1		2		
			8	3	5			
		5					8	2
			5		2			
7	6					9		
			1	7	6			
		1		5			2	6
	9					5		

Our first goal is to quickly and easily fill in as many blank squares as possible **before having to determine all the possibilities for that square**.

Step 1:

To quickly fill in the grid I begin by looking for **pairs of numbers** along horizontal lines in rows 1-3, then 4-6 and finally 7-9.

To add order to this method I begin with the lowest numbers and work my way up to the highest numbers (rather than working on the first numbers my eyes happen to catch).

		8					3	
4	5	3		1		2		
←			8	3	5			
		5					8	2
			5		2			
7	6					9		
			1	7	6			
		1		5			2	6
	9					5		

Starting with the number '1' I notice that my first pair is '3'. By eliminating the 1st and 3rd rows I see that I can place a '3' in row 2, column 3.

For clarity, numbers that are added to the original grid will have an underline.

Elimination like this is a fairly standard approach so let's work through this part quickly. In the first 3 rows we also have a pair of 5's and 8's. Let's work through those.

		8				↑	3	5
4	5	3		1		2		→
			8	3	5			→
		5					8	2
			5		2			
7	6					9		
			1	7	6			
		1		5			2	6
	9					5		

For the 5's I see that I have a pair of 5's (one in 2nd row and one in the 3rd row) and a third '5' in the 9th row and 7th column.

This eliminates all but one open square in Box #3 so I can place a '5' in the 1st row 9th column. Notice the new '5' in the first row is underlined.

For the 8's I see that I have a pair in rows 1 and 3 and another in 4th row, 8th column. This eliminates all the possibilities for Box #3 except the 2nd row and 9th column.

		8					3	5
4	5	3		1		2		8
			8	3	5			
		5					8	2
			5		2			
7	6					9		
			1	7	6			
		1		5			2	6
	9					5		

Now we are finished with the first 3 rows.

Let's work through the next 3 rows in the same manner.

We have two 2's and two 5's. Using the same type of elimination we can add two more numbers to the grid.

Here's how we add the '2'.

		8					3	5
4	5	3		1		2		8
			8	3	5			
←		5					8	2
←			5		2			
7	6	2				9		
			1	7	6			
		1		5			2	6
	9					5		

Here's how we add the '5'.

		8					3	5
4	5	3		1		2		8
			8	3	5			
		5				→	8	2
			5		2			→
7	6	2				9	5	↓
			1	7	6			
		1		5			2	6
	9					5		

Please notice that the new '5' was added because we added a '5' in row 1, column 9. This is an important point.

Whenever you add a new number, take a moment to see if you can add more because you have filled in something new. I'll come back to that later.

That's all we can do for rows 4-6.

Let's move on to rows 7-9.

I have a pair of 1's but can't eliminate all of the open spaces. I have a pair of 6's but can't eliminate all the open spaces for 6's either.

I have a pair of 5's in rows 8 and 9, and a pair of 5's in columns 1-3. That completely eliminates all the possibilities except one.

		8					3	5
4	5	3		1		2		8
			8	3	5			
		5					8	2
			5		2			
7	6	2				9	5	
5			1	7	6			
		1		5			2	6
	9					5		

At this point we are finished with analyzing the rows. Now we'll move on to the columns.

To make it easier to see where we're adding numbers because of column elimination I've removed the underlining from the numbers we added while examining the rows.

Step 2:

Now I am looking for pairs along vertical lines in columns
1-3, then 4-6 and finally 7-9.

		8					3	5
4	5	3		1		2		8
			8	3	5			
		5					8	2
			5		2			
7	6	2				9	5	
5			1	7	6			
		1		5			2	6
	9					5		

Unfortunately, we don't have any pairs in columns 1-3 (we
have three 5's so we don't need to do anything with 5's).

Let's look at columns 4-6. We have a pair of 1's but we
can't eliminate enough open spaces. That's all we have for
pairs in columns 4-6 so let's look at columns 7-9.

In columns 7-9 we have a pair of 8's but we can't eliminate
enough open spaces to fill in the 3rd eight.

At this point we are finished with Step #2.

Step 3:

Now I look for what I call 'Alleys'. These are Boxes that
have 3 consecutive open squares along either the horizontal
or vertical with most of the other numbers identified in that
Box. I see an Alley in Box 1 in the 3rd row.

		8					3	5
4	5	3		1		2		8
			8	3	5			
		5					8	2
			5		2			
7	6	2				9	5	
5			1	7	6			
		1		5			2	6
	9					5		

Box 1 has three consecutive open spaces in the 3rd row that
might help me fill in one of the open squares in the 1st row
of Box 1. By using a number in the 3rd row from Box 2 or
3, all I have to do is find the same number from the 3rd row
in the 1st or 2nd column of Box 4 or 7. This is the concept
of Alleys. Unfortunately the numbers in the 3rd row ('3',
'5', '8') are already identified in Box 1. Likewise we have
an Alley in the 1st Row of Box 2 that doesn't yield any
results. Although we have other Alleys in this puzzle, none
produce any additional numbers.

Because Alleys are such an important concept I'd like to step through a couple of examples <u>not in our puzzle</u>.

Alleys provide easy solutions without examining all the possibilities.

	2	8					3	
4	5	3		6	9	2		7
			1	2	3			

This is an Alley in the 1st Box because you have 3 open squares in a row and most of the rest of the Box filled in. I know that a '1' must go in the 1st Row, 1st Column because the '1' in the 2nd Box eliminates any other possibility.

Here's another example. This is an Alley in the 2nd Box. Even though you don't have a pair of 8's you can eliminate all other possibilities for '8' in the 2nd Box. The '8' must go in the 2nd Row, 4th Column.

	2	8					3	
4	5	3		6	9	2		7
			1	2	3			

Alleys can be either vertical or horizontal. You may need to use a number from another box to completely eliminate all other possibilities.

Step 4:

Now I look for rows, columns and Boxes where I can easily
spot most or all of the numbers 1-9.

		8					3	5
4	5	3		1		2		8
			8	3	5			
		5					8	2
			5		2			
7	6	2				9	5	
5		4	1	7	6			
		1		5			2	6
	9					5		

For example, look at the square in the 7th row and 3rd
column. By examining all the numbers in the 7th Box, 7th
row **and** 3rd column I can eliminate all but the number 4.
Do you see how you can find all the numbers 1 through 9
except 4?

For this step in the process I like to start with the number
'1' and count to '9'. In this case the number '1' is in both
the 7th row and 4th column and in the 7th Box.

Now that we've filled in that '4' the 7th row has only 4 open spaces. Look at the square in the 7th row 8th column.

		8					3	5
4	5	3		1		2		8
			8	3	5			
		5					8	2
			5		2			
7	6	2				9	5	
5		4	1	7	6		9	
		1		5			2	6
	9					5		

You can eliminate all the numbers except '9'.

Remember how I said whenever you add a number you need to see if by adding that number you can add another and we'd come back to it later. Now is a good time to examine that.

		8				↑	3	5
4	5	3		1		2	↑	8
			8	3	5			9
		5					8	2
			5		2			
7	6	2				9	5	
5		4	1	7	6		9	
		1		5			2	6
	9					5		

By adding the '4' in Box 7 it doesn't eliminate all the open spaces. But, by adding the '9' in Box 9 it does eliminate all the open spaces in Box 3. We can add a '9' in the 3rd row and 9th column.

By adding the '9' to the 3rd Box it eliminates all the open spaces for a '9' in Box 1.

9	↑	8					3	5
4	5	3		1		2		8
←			8	3	5			9
		5					8	2
			5		2			
7	6	2				9	5	
5		4	1	7	6		9	
		1		5			2	6
	9					5		

Likewise by adding the '9' to Box 1 it eliminates all the open spaces for a '9' in Box 4.

9	↑	8					3	5
4	5	3		1		2		8
			8	3	5			9
		5					8	2
		9	5		2			
7	6	2				9	5	
5		4	1	7	6		9	
		1		5			2	6
▼	9					5		

We had a good run on the 9's. I've had puzzles that allowed me to fill in all the same number on the grid using this method. Unfortunately, we can't fill in any more 9's using this step.

At this point I also like to check and see if there are any new Alleys.

Since I don't see any we'll move on to Step 5.

Step 5:

Now I want to start identifying possibilities. I look for
rows, columns and Boxes where most of the numbers are
already filled in. Look at column 3. There are only 2 blank
squares.

9		8					3	5
4	5	3		1		2		8
		6 7	8	3	5			9
		5					8	2
		9	5		2			
7	6	2				9	5	
5		4	1	7	6		9	
		1		5			2	6
	9	6 7				5		

The last two numbers for the 3rd column are '6' and '7'.
Neither of those numbers can be eliminated with the
information we have. Now is the time we begin to write
down the possibilities in the squares. In small print, write 6
7 in each of the open Boxes in the 3rd column.

Whenever we are down to two possibilities for two squares,
in this case '6' & '7', we call that a 'twin'. Let's take an
in-depth look at this concept.

As an example, below is a row from a puzzle. We have a
twin '1' & '4' in the last two squares.

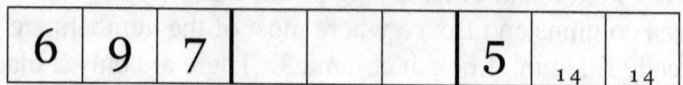

<u>If those are the only possibilities for those two squares</u> then
I know that '1' and '4' must go in those two squares.

<u>I don't know which one goes where</u>, but I do know that I
can't have a '1' or '4' in any of the other open squares in
that row.

Do you see how that works? This is the concept of twins.

The same would be true if I had three squares and only
three possibilities for each of those three squares, which
would be a triplet. The following is an example of a triplet.

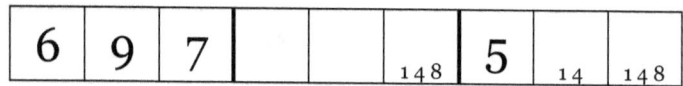

Again, I don't know which number goes where, but I do
know that I can't have a '1', '4' or '8' in any other blank
square in that row.

Here's an example of a quad.

There are four squares and four possibilities. In this case I
know that the open square must contain a '3' because all
other numbers have been eliminated.

Now back to our puzzle.

Look at the 2nd row. There are only 3 open spaces for numbers '6', '7' and '9'. All three numbers work in the 2nd row, 4th column. Only '7' and '9' work in the 6th column because of the '6' in the 7th row. Only the '6' and '7' work in the 8th column because of the '9' in the 3rd Box.

9		8		1		2		3	5
4	5	3	6 7 9		7 9		6 7	8	
		6 7	8	3	5			9	
		5					8	2	
		9	5		2				
7	6	2				9	5		
5		4	1	7	6		9		
		1		5			2	6	
	9	6 7				5			

As we eliminate numbers **we'll cross out the small numbers that represent possibilities** until we have only one possibility remaining.

When we have only one possibility remaining in a square, we can enter the number that belongs in that square.

Look at the 7th row. There are only 3 open squares for the numbers '2', '3' and '8'. The '2' can't go in either of the open squares in the 9th Box so it must go in the only open square left in the 7th row and that is the 2nd column.

9		8					3	5
4	5	3	6 7 9	1	7 9	2	6 7	8
	6 7		8	3	5			9
		5					8	2
		9	5		2			
7	6	2				9	5	
5	2	4	1	7	6	8	9	3
		1		5			2	6
	9	6 7				5		

That leaves us with only two numbers for the 7th row, numbers '3' and '8'. Since we have '8' in the 2nd row, 9th column it means the '8' must go in the 7th column. That leaves only one open square in the 7th row, that means the '3' must go in the 9th column.

Now that we've filled in some new numbers it is time to go back and see if those numbers reveal additional numbers.

9	5	8					3	5
4	5	3	6 7 9	1	7 9	2	6 7	8
2		6 7	8	3	5			9
		5					8	2
		9	5		2			
7	6	2				9	5	
5	2	4	1	7	6	8	9	3
		1		5			2	6
	9	6 7				5		

Looking at the 2's in the 2nd and 3rd columns shows us that we can eliminate all the open spaces in the 1st Box except the open square in the 1st column, 3rd row.

The '8' and '3' in the 7th row don't eliminate all the numbers in the other Boxes so let's go back to filling in possibilities starting with the rows, columns and Boxes with the most numbers in them.

The 1st Box has only 3 open squares for numbers '1', '6' and '7'. The '6' can't go in either open square in the 2nd column because of the '6' in the 6th row. That leaves us with '6' as the only number left for the 3rd row, 3rd column.

9	↑	8					3	5
4	5	3	679	1	79	2	67	8
2		6	8	3	5			9
		5					8	2
		9	5		2			
7	6	2				9	5	
5	2	4	1	7	6	8	9	3
		1		5			2	6
	9	6 7				5		

With a '6' in the 1st Box it means that the '6' in the 7th Box is eliminated leaving only the '7' for the 9th row, 3rd column.

Let's go back to see if our new entries have provided us with any clues for the remaining open squares.

Plugging in the '6' and '7' in the 3rd column leaves only one open square for a '6' in the 9th row, 1st column. Let's plug that '6' in now in the 9th row, 1st column.

9		8					3	5
4	5	3	6 7 9	1	7 9	2	6 7	8
2		6	8	3	5			9
		5					8	2
		9	5		2			
7	6	2				9	5	
5	2	4	1	7	6	8	9	3
		1		5		7	2	6
6	9	7				5		

The '7' in the 7th Box leaves us with only one open square in the 9th Box.

This new '7' in the 9th Box and this new '6' in the 9th row, 1st column don't provide us with any new numbers.

Let's go back to filling in possibilities.

The 1st Box has only two open squares for the numbers '1' and '7'. We have another twin.

The 9th Box has only two open squares for the numbers '1' and '4'. It is another twin.

9 (17)	8					↑	3	5
4	5	3	(679)	1	(79)	2	(67)	8
2 (17)	6	8	3	5	(14)	(147)		9
	5						8	2
	9		5		2			
7	6	2				9	5	
5	2	4	1	7	6	8	9	3
		1		5		7	2	6
6	9	7 (6)				5	(14)	(14)

The 3rd row has only three open squares for the numbers '1', '4' and '7'. The '4' can't go in the 1st Box because there's already a '4' there and the '7' can't go in the 7th column because of the '7' in the 8th row, 7th column.

None of these has eliminated numbers so we continue to fill in possibilities.

The 9th column has only 3 open squares for numbers '1', '4' and '7'. Notice that the '7' can't go in the 6th row or the 9th row which leaves only one open square for the '7', that's the 5th row, 9th column.

Using our new number '7' doesn't provide us with any new Alleys or elimination by horizontal or vertical pairs.

9 ₁₇	8						3	5
4	5	3 ₆₇₉		1 ₇₉		2 ₆₇		8
2 ₁₇		6	8	3	5 ₁₄		147	9
		5					8	2
		9	5		2			7
7	6	2				9	5 ₁₄	→
5	2	4	1	7	6	8	9	3
38	38	1		5		7	2	6
6	9	6 7				5 ₁₄		14 →

There are 2 open squares in the 7th Box for numbers '3' and '8'. That leaves us with a twin '3' and '8' as the only possibilities left for the 7th Box.

Again, twins are useful for eliminating possibilities, as we'll see in a moment.

The 1st column has three open squares for numbers '1', '3' and '8'. The 4th row has an '8' in the 8th column so the only possibilities for the square in the 4th row and 1st column are '1' and '3'.

9 (17)	8						3	5
4	5	3	(679)	1	(79)	2	(67)	8
2 (17)	6	8	3	5	(14)	(147)		9
(13)		5					8	2
(138)		9	5		2			7
7	6	2				9	5	(14)
5	2	4	1	7	6	8	9	3
(38)	(38)	1		5		7	2	6
6	9	(6) 7				5	(14)	(14)

All three of the possibilities work for the 5th row in the 1st column.

At this point we are out of Boxes with only 3 numbers missing. It is worth noting that it is often easy to miss other rows, columns or Boxes with only 3 open squares so examine your puzzle carefully.

Before we move on to Boxes with 4 open squares, take a
moment to go back to Steps 1-4 to see if you can quickly
fill in any more numbers. I don't see any, do you?

9 ₁₇	8					3	5
4	5	3 ₆₇₉	1 ₇₉	2 ₆₇	8		
2 ₁₇	6	8	3	5 ₁₄	₁₄₇	9	
₁₃	5				8	2	
₁₃₈	9	5	2			7	
7	6	2			9	5 ₁₄	
5	2	4	1	7	6	8	9	3
₃₈ ₃₈	1 ₄₉	5 ₄₉	7	2	6	
6	9 ₆7			5 ₁₄	₁₄	

Before moving onto Boxes, I want to illustrate another
important concept of using twins for eliminating
possibilities.

Notice that there are 4 open squares in the 8th row. We've
identified two of them as having a twin, two possibilities
'3' and '8' for the first two squares in the 8th row. That
means the remaining two squares in the 8th row MUST BE
either '4' or '9'.

Take a moment to make sure you see this, as we'll use this
important concept again and again.

Now let's start with Box 1 and work our way to Box 9 looking for 4 open squares. There are 4 open squares in Box 3 for numbers '1', '4', '6' and '7'. We've filled in three of the four open squares. The last open square in the 1st row, 7th column must contain '1', '4' and '6' as possibilities because of the '7' in the 8th row.

9 (17)		8		1		1 4 6	3	5
4	5	3 (679)		1 (79)		2 (67)		8
2 (17)		6	8	3	5	(1 4)	(1 4 7)	9
(13)	(134)	5					8	2
(138)	(1348)	9	5		2			7
7	6	2				9	5 (14)	
5	2	4	1	7	6	8	9	3
(38)	(38)	1 (49)	5	(49)		7	2	6
6	9	₆7				5 (14)	(14)	

There are four open squares in Box 4 with numbers '1', '3', '4' and '8' as possibilities. There's already '8' in the 4th row and '4' in the 1st column leaving us with the possibilities above.

Do you recall the twins in the 7th Box? Twins are two
possible numbers in two squares ('3' and '8' in 7th Box).
We have that situation again. The '1' and '7' in the 1st Box
eliminate the possibility of having a '1' or '7' any other
place in 2nd column.

9 17	8			146	3	5
4	5	3 679	1 79	2 67		8
2 17		6	8	3	5 14	147	9
13	*34	5				8	2
138	*348	9	5	2			7
7	6	2			9	5 14	
5	2	4	1	7	6	8	9	3
38	38	1 49	5 49	7	2	6
6	9	67			5 14	14	

You can eliminate the 1's in the 4th Box, 2nd column
because you have twins of 1 & 7 in the 1st Box.

Because the concept of twins works in a variety of ways,
I'm going to go over this situation again.

You MUST have a `1' and a '7' in the 1st Box – at this
point we don't know which goes where. But the 2nd
column in Box 1 must have a '1' and a '7' which eliminates
the possibility of having a '1' or '7' in the 2nd column of
Box #4.

We have four open squares in the 6th Box with possible numbers of '1', '3', '4' and '6'.

9 (17)	8					(146)	3	5
4	5	3	(679)	1	(79)	2	(67)	8
2 (17)		6	8	3	5	(14)	(147)	9
(13)	(‡34)	5				(1346)	8	2
(138)	(‡348)	9	5		2	(1346)	(146)	7
7	6	2	(34)	(48)	(1348)	9	5	(14)
5	2	4	1	7	6	8	9	3
(38)	(38)	1	(49)	5	(49)	7	2	6
6	9	₆7				5	(14)	(14)

That's all of the Boxes with four open squares that haven't been filled in with possibilities. Let's look at the rows next.

The 6th row has four open squares with possible numbers '1', '3', '4' and '8'. By now you should be able to understand what the possibilities are and why so I've simply listed them above.

I don't see any pairs that would eliminate numbers. Remember, just as you can have pairs (twins) you can have three-of-a-kind (triplets) and four-of-a-kind (quads).

By starting with Boxes, rows and columns with 3 or 4 open squares we were hoping to identify as many numbers as possible <u>before going through every open square</u> to identify the possibilities. Since we can't fill in any more squares the time has come to fill in the rest of the possibilities.

9 (17)	8	(2467)	(246)	(47)	(146)	3	5	
4	5	3 (679)	1	(79)	2	(67)	8	
2 (17)	6	8	3	5	(14)	(147)	9	
(13)	(≠34)	5	(34679)	(469)	(13479)	(1346)	8	2
(138)	(≠348)	9	5	(468)	2	(1346)	(146)	7
7	6	2	(34)	(48)	(1348)	9	5	(14)
5	2	4	1	7	6	8	9	3
(38)	(38)	1	(49)	5	(49)	7	2	6
6	9	↙7	(23)	(28)	(38)	5	(14)	(14)

In the 9th row the three open squares in the 4th, 5th and 6th column can't be either '4' or '9' because those numbers are already 'paired' as twins in the 8th row of the 8th Box. Neither can those squares contain a '1' because of the twins in the 9th row of the 9th Box.

Now all the possibilities have been identified. It is time to do some thinking.

Step 6:

It is time to look for 4 different occurrences.
   a) Numbers that only occur once in a Box, row or
      column.
   b) Twins that eliminate possibilities.
   c) Triplets that eliminate possibilities.
   d) Quads that eliminate possibilities

I prefer to do them in the order listed above. Let's look for
numbers that only occur once in a Box first.

9 $_{17}$	8	2467	246	47	146	3	5	
4	5	3 $_{679}$	1	79	2	67	8	
2 $_{17}$	6	8	3	5 $_{14}$	147	9		
13	≠34	5 $_{34679}$	469	13479	1346	8	2	
138	≠348	9	5 $_{468}$	2	1346	146	7	
7	6	2 $_{34}$	48	1348	9	5 $_{14}$		
5	2	4	1	7	6	8	9	3
38	38	1 $_{49}$	5	49	7	2	6	
6	9 $_{6}$7	23	28	38	5 $_{14}$	14		

The Boxes do not appear to have any numbers that appear
only once in a Box.

The rows do not appear to have any numbers that appear
only once in a Box.

In the 5th column I see only one possibility for the number '9' and that's in the 4th row and 5th column.

9 17	8	2467	246	47	146	3	5
4	5	3	679	1	79	2	67	8
2 17	6	8	3	5	14	147	9
13	ǂ34	5	34679	~~9~~ 9	13479	1346	8	2
138	ǂ348	9	5	468	2	1346	146	7
7	6	2	34	48	1348	9	5	14
5	2	4	1	7	6	8	9	3
38	38	1	49	5	49	7	2	6
6	9	6 7	23	28	38	5	14	14

At this point you can eliminate all the other possibilities for '9' in that Box, row and column.

<u>It is very important that you consistently eliminate possibilities as numbers are identified.</u> You may be tempted to jump ahead and start filling in numbers as they have been identified before you have crossed out the numbers that have been eliminated. Don't do it. Cross out all the eliminated possibilities before moving on. I like to cross out the eliminated possibilities in the effected Box, then the row and then the column, in that order.

I've crossed out the 9's in the 5th Box above.

From this point forward I also go through steps 1-4 for every new number I identify.

9 ₁₇	8	2467	246	47	146	3	5
4	5	3 ₆₇₉	1	79	2	67	8
2 ₁₇	6	8	3	5	14	147	9
13	⁺34	5	34679	⁺6 9	13479	1346	8	2
138	⁺348	9	5	468	2	1346	146	7
7	6	2	34	48	1348	9	5	14
5	2	4	1	7	6	8	9	3
38	38	1	49	5	49	7	2	6
6	9	₆7	23	28	38	5	14	14

- The columns do not appear to have any more instances where a number occurs only once.
- I don't see any twins that eliminate possibilities.
- I don't see any triplets that eliminate possibilities.
- I don't see any quads that eliminate possibilities.

It is at this point that most people give up.

For us, it is time to move on to Step 7.

Step 7:

It is time to analyze situations where a set of numbers eliminates another number based upon the position of those numbers on the grid.

9 (17)	8	(2467)	(246)	(47)	(146)	3	5
4	5	3 (679)	1	(79)	2	(67)	8
2 (17)	6	8	3	5 (14)	(147)	9	
(13) (‡34)	5	(‰4679)	(‡69)	(1‰479)	(1346)	8	2
(138) (‡348)	9	5	(468)	2	(1346)	(146)	7
7 6	2 (34)	(48)	(1348)	9	5	(14)	
5	2	4	1	7	6	8	9	3
(38) (38)	1	(49)	5	(49)	7	2	6
6 9	(‰7)	(23)	(28)	(38)	5	(14)	(14)

Look at the 4th Box. The only 8's in Box 4 are found in the 5th row. That means there can be no other 8's in the 5th row because the 4th Box MUST HAVE '8'. Therefore we can eliminate the '8' in the 5th column, 5th row.

Look at the 6th row. The only 3's are in the 5th Box. Since the 6th row must have 3's, there can be no other 3's in the 5th Box other than those in the 6th row. So we can eliminate the 3's in the 4th row, 4th column and the 4th row, 6th column.

Now that we've eliminated those numbers let's go back and quickly repeat Step 6 a-d.

9 17	**8**	2467	246	47	146	**3**	**5**	
4	**5**	**3** 679	**1**	79	**2**	67	**8**	
2 17	**6**	**8**	**3**	**5** 14	147	**9**		
13	34	**5**	34679	69	19479	1346	**8**	**2**
138	348	**9**	**5**	468	**2**	1346	146	**7**
7	**6**	**2**	34	48	3 8	**9**	**5**	14
5	**2**	**4**	**1**	**7**	**6**	**8**	**9**	**3**
38	38	**1**	49	**5**	49	**7**	**2**	**6**
6	**9**	7	23	28	38	**5**	14	14

At some point in your working through your puzzle you will notice that you have several choices to choose from for your next step. This is one of those times.

If the puzzle is properly constructed, it shouldn't make any difference what order you decide to pursue. You should end up with the same answer regardless of the order with which you've approached the solution.

For example, in our current puzzle you'll notice that you have both a triplet and a quad in the 6th column.

Let's go over this concept in detail to be certain you understand it.

The triplet is '4', '7' & '9' from the 1st, 2nd and 8th rows of the 6th column.

Those three squares MUST CONTAIN '4', '7' and '9'. We don't know which square will contain which number but we know those three numbers are the numbers for those three squares.

That means we can eliminate '4', '7' and '9' from any other square in the 6th column. Don't do it just yet because I want to review the quad first.

For the quad the possibilities are:
1st row are '4' & '7'
2nd row has '7' & '9'
4th row has '1', '4' & '7'
8th row has '4' & '9'.

Taken together those four squares MUST CONTAIN the numbers '1', '4', '7' & '9'.

That means we can eliminate those four numbers from the rest of the squares in the 6th column.

Using either approach the triple or the quad, is fine and will lead you to the same solution. The only difference is that one approach may result in a quicker solution. I don't often see a quad so we'll go in that direction.

Specifically we will eliminate '1' & '4' from the 6th row, 6th column leaving us with only '3' & '8' as possibilities in that square.

Let's see how changing the 6th column has affected the 6th row.

We now have only one '1' in the 6th row and it's in the 9th column so we can place a '1' in the 6th row, 9th column. At this point we need to eliminate all the 1's in the 6th Box, 6th row and 9th column.

9 ₁₇	8	2467	246	47	146	3	5
4	5	3 ₆₇₉	1	79	2 ₆₇	8	
2 ₁₇	6	8	3	5	14	≠47	9
13 ≠34	5	≠4679 ≠69	19479 ≠346	8	2		
138 ≠348	9	5	468	2	≠346 ≠46	7	
7	6	2 34	48	≠3≠8	9	5	≠1
5	2	4	1	7	6	8	9	3
38	38	1 49	5	49	7	2	6
6	9 ₆7	23	28	38	5	≠1	≠4

The '1' in the 6th row eliminates the possibility of a '1' in the 9th column. So we can place a '4' in the 9th row, 9th column. Remember to eliminate possibilities because of the new '4'.

The '4' in the 9th row eliminates the possibility of a '4' in the 8th column. So we can place a '1' in the 9th row, 8th column. Eliminate possibilities because of the new '1'.

Eliminating the '1' in the 5th row, 8th column reveals a new twin in the 5th row. Do you see it?

The pair of possibilities in the 5th row, 5th column and 5th row, 8th column is both '4' & '6'. That means '4' & '6' can't appear anywhere else in the 5th row so we can eliminate those other possibilities. When we eliminate the 4's and 6's in the other squares in the 5th row we see that the 7th column has only one number left '3'. Remember to eliminate possibilities because of the new number.

9 ₁₇	**8**	2467	246	47	146	**3**	**5**	
4	**5**	**3**	679	**1**	79	**2**	67	**8**
2 ₁₇	**6**	**8**	**3**	**5**	14	~~4~~ 47	**9**	
~~3~~	~~3~~4	**5**	~~9~~4679	~~6~~ **9**	19479	~~9~~46	**8**	**2**
1 ~~38~~	~~34~~8	**9**	**5**	468	**2**	**3** ~~46~~	~~4~~46	**7**
7	**6**	**2**	34	48	~~3~~~~8~~	**9**	**5**	~~1~~
5	**2**	**4**	**1**	**7**	**6**	**8**	**9**	**3**
38	38	**1**	49	**5**	49	**7**	**2**	**6**
6	**9**	~~7~~	23	28	38	**5**	~~1~~	~~4~~

Eliminating the '1' in the 5th row also leaves us with only one '1' in the 5th row, which you see in the 1st column. Go ahead and plug the '1' in the 1st column 5th row.

Remember to always eliminate possibilities because of the new numbers.

At this point we have a solution for 2 more squares. We know the 4th row, 1st column is '3' and we know the 5th row, 2nd column is '8'. I prefer to work from the top down so we'll plug in the '3'.

9 17	8	2467	246	47	146	3	5
4	5	3	679	1	79	2	67	8
2 17	6	8	3	5	14	≠47	9
≠3	≠94	5	94679	≠69	19479	≠946	8	2
1̲38	≠348	9	5	468	2	≠3≠6	≠46	7
7	6	2	34	48	≠3≠8	9	5	≠1̲
5	2	4	1	7	6	8	9	3
98	38	1	49	5	49	7	2	6
6	9	67	23	28	38	5	≠1̲	≠4̲

Remember to eliminate possibilities because of the new '3'.

Eliminating those possibilities reveals the solution for two more squares. We now know that the 4th row, 2nd column must be '4' and the 8th row, 1st column must be '8'.

Working from the top down, let's plug in the '4' in the 4th Box before moving on to the others.

Plugging in the '4' in the 4th row, 2nd column and eliminating all the other 4's in the 4th row shows us that the 4th row, 7th column can only be '6'. Since that is our topmost known square let's plug it in now.

9	17	8	2467	246	47	146	3	5
4	5	3	679	1	79	2	67	8
2	17	6	8	3	5	14	47	9
3	4	5	34679	9	13479	6	8	2
1	38	9	5	468	2	3	46	7
7	6	2	34	48	38	9	5	1
5	2	4	1	7	6	8	9	3
8	38	1	49	5	49	7	2	6
6	9	7	23	28	38	5	1	4

By plugging '6' in the 4th row, 7th column we've revealed two more solutions. The first is the 4th row and 4th column – it must be '7'. The second is the 5th row and 8th column – it must be '4'.

Before we plug those numbers in, I want to draw your attention to the twin in Box 3. The 7th column has '1' & '4' as possibilities for the 1st & 3rd rows.

As you know a twin means we can eliminate all other possibilities for '1' and '4' in Box 3. By doing so we see that the 3rd row, 8th column has only '7' left as a possible solution. Because that is the topmost known square let's plug that in now.

After plugging in the '7' be sure to eliminate all the possibilities for 7's in the 3rd Box, 3rd row and 8th column.

9	17	8	2467	246	47	146	3	5
4	5	3	679	1	79	2	6₇	8
2	17	6	8	3	5	14	7	9
3	4	5	34679	9	13479	6	8	2
1	38	9	5	468	2	3 46	46	7
7	6	2	34	48	348	9	5	1
5	2	4	1	7	6	8	9	3
8	38	1	49	5	49	7	2	6
6	9	7	23	28	38	5	1	4

Eliminating the 7's reveals two more squares with only one number left. They are the '6' in the 2nd row, 8th column and the '1' in the 3rd row, 2nd column.

Let's plug in the '6' and eliminate all the other possibilities for 6's in the 3rd Box, 2nd row and 8th column.

Eliminating the '6' in the 2nd Box reveals another twin, the '7' & '9' in 2nd row, 4th & 6th columns.

The pair of '7' & '9' in the 2nd row eliminates both '7' and '9' in the 2nd Box. We don't have any other 9's but we do have two 7's we can eliminate. Eliminating the '7' in the 6th column provides us with another square with only a single possibility, the '4' in the 1st row, 6th column. Let's plug that in now.

9	±7	8	2±6⅋	2±6	4⅋	1±6	3	5
4	5	3	₆79	1	79	2	6⅋	8
2	1⅋	6	8	3	5	±4	±±7	9
±3	±₃4	5	₃₄679	±₆9	1₃479	±₃±6	8	2
1₃₈	±₃±8	9	5	468	2	±3±6	±46	7
7	6	2	34	48	±3±8	9	5	±1
5	2	4	1	7	6	8	9	3
₃8	38	1	49	5	±9	7	2	6
6	9	₆7	23	28	38	5	±1	±4

Eliminating the other 4's reveals two more squares with only one possibility left. They are the '1' in the 1st row & 7th column and the '9' in the 8th row & 6th column.

Working from the top, let's plug in the '1' in the 1st row, 7th column and eliminate the other possibilities of '1' in the 3rd Box, 1st row and 7th column.

Eliminating 1's reveals two more squares where there is only one possibility, the 1st row, 2nd column and the 3rd row, 7th column.

Working from the top let's plug in the '7' in the 1st row, 2nd column and then eliminate the other 7's.

9	₹7	8	2₹6₹	2₹6	4₹	1₹6	3	5
4	5	3	679	1	79	2	6₹	8
2	1₹	6	8	3	5	₹4	₹₹7	9
₹3	₹9 4	5	9₹679	₹6 9	19479	₹9₹6	8	2
1₹9₹8	₹9₹8	9	5	468	2	₹3₹6	₹46	7
7	6	2	34	48	₹3₹8	9	5	₹1
5	2	4	1	7	6	8	9	3
₹8	38	1	49	5	₹9	7	2	6
6	9	₹7	23	28	38	5	₹1	₹4

I see several Boxes that have only one square left as well as squares that have only one solution left.

Because speed is one of our primary objectives we'll proceed by plugging in numbers that are already solved before going back to finding pairs etc.

Let's plug the numbers in the Boxes with only one number left and continue eliminating possibilities based upon that.

In Box 1 we'll place '1' and eliminate other possibilities.
In Box 3 we'll place '4' and eliminate other possibilities.
In Box 4 we'll place '8' and eliminate other possibilities.
In Box 6 we'll place '4' and eliminate other possibilities.

There are many ways to solve this puzzle from here. For example you could plug the '2' in the 2nd Box or the '7' in the 5th Box. It doesn't matter which way you proceed, you will end up with the same solution.

9	*7	8	2 4 6 9	2 4 6	4*	1 4 6	3	5
4	5	3	6 7 9	1	7 9	2	6*	8
2	1*	6	8	3	5	*4	**7	9
*3	**4	5	9 4 6 7 9	*9	1 9 4 7 9	*3*6	8	2
1**	**8	9	5	*6*	2	*3*6	*4*	7
7	6	2	3 4	4 8	*3*8	9	5	*1
5	2	4	1	7	6	8	9	3
*8	3*	1	4 9	5	*9	7	2	6
6	9	*7	2 3	2 8	3 8	5	*1	*4

I see the 5th row has only one open square. Let's plug in a '6' and eliminate possibilities.

I see all the numbers have been used except one in the 1st and 2nd columns. Let's plug those numbers in the 1st and 2nd columns and eliminate possibilities.

In the 1st row, 5th column the only possibility left is '2'. We'll plug that in and eliminate other possible 2's.

9	₊7	8	₂₄6₇	2₄₆	4₇	1₄₆	3	5
4	5	3	6₇9	1	79	2	6₇	8
2	1₇	6	8	3	5	₊4	₊₄7	9
₊3	₊₉4	5	₃₄6₇9	₄₆9	19479	₊₉₄6	8	2
1₃₈	₊₉₄8	9	5	₊6₈	2	₊3₄₆	₊4₆	7
7	6	2	34	48	₊3₄8	9	5	₊1
5	2	4	1	7	6	8	9	3
₉8	3₈	1	49	5	₊9	7	2	6
6	9	₆7	23	₂8	38	5	₊1	₊4

Now we have only one open square in the 1st row. For the first row all of the numbers '1' through '9' have been used except '6'. Let's plug a '6' in the 1st row, 4th column and continue eliminating possibilities.

In the 4th row, 4th column we have only one solution for that square, '7'.

Plugging '7' in the 4th row, 4th column left us with only one possibility in the 2nd row, 4th column and that would be '9'. Let's plug it in and eliminate possibilities.

9	₊7	8	₂₄6₋	2₄₆	4₋	1₄₆	3	5
4	5	3	₆₋9	1	7₉	2	6₋	8
2	1₋	6	8	3	5	₊4	₊₄7	9
₊3	₊₉4	5	₃₄₆7₉	₄₆9	1₃₄₇₉	₊₃₄6	8	2
1₃₈	₁₃₄8	9	5	₊6₈	2	₊3₄₆	₊4₆	7
7	6	2	3₄	48	₊3₄8	9	5	₊1
5	2	4	1	7	6	8	9	3
₉8	3₈	1	4₉	5	₊9	7	2	6
6	9	₆7	23	₉8	38	5	₊1	₊4

We have only one open square in the 2nd row. Plug in '7' and eliminate possibilities.

We have only one open square in the 4th row. Plug in '1' and eliminate possibilities.

We have only one possibility for the 8th row, 4th column and that would be '4'. Plug in '4' and eliminate possibilities.

That leaves us with only one possibility for the square in the 6th row, 4th column and that would be '3'. Plug in a '3' and eliminate possibilities.

9	7	8	6	2	4	1	3	5
4	5	3	9	1	7	2	6	8
2	1	6	8	3	5	4	7	9
3	4	5	7	9	1	6	8	2
1	8	9	5	6	2	3	4	7
7	6	2	3	4	8	9	5	1
5	2	4	1	7	6	8	9	3
8	3	1	4	5	9	7	2	6
6	9	7	2	8	3	5	1	4

That leaves us with only one possibility for the 6th row, 6th column and that would be '8'. Plug it in an eliminate possibilities.

We have only one open square in the 6th and 8th rows. Plug in '4' and '9' and eliminate possibilities.

We are left with only one open square in each of the columns 4 through 6. Plug in '2', '8' and '3' and congratulations the puzzle is complete. I know it wasn't easy. I hope you learned the methodology because we are going to tackle an even more challenging puzzle next.

More Definitions

To speed up this process we'll use the following shorthand
to identify the individual squares.

R1C1	R1C2	R1C3	R1C4	R1C5	R1C6	R1C7	R1C8	R1C9
R2C1	R2C2	R2C3	R2C4	R2C5	R2C6	R2C7	R2C8	R2C9
R3C1	R3C2	R3C3	R3C4	R3C5	R3C6	R3C7	R3C8	R3C9
R4C1	R4C2	R4C3	R4C4	R4C5	R4C6	R4C7	R4C8	R4C9
R5C1	R5C2	R5C3	R5C4	R5C5	R5C6	R5C7	R5C8	R5C9
R6C1	R6C2	R6C3	R6C4	R6C5	R6C6	R6C7	R6C8	R6C9
R7C1	R7C2	R7C3	R7C4	R7C5	R7C6	R7C7	R7C8	R7C9
R8C1	R8C2	R8C3	R8C4	R8C5	R8C6	R8C7	R8C8	R8C9
R9C1	R9C2	R9C3	R9C4	R9C5	R9C6	R9C7	R9C8	R9C9

The 'R' stands for the row and the 'C' stands for the
column.

Also, the possibilities for each square will simply be listed
as numbers. For example 46 would mean there are two
possibilities '4' and '6'.

Puzzle #2

You'll need a fresh 8.5" x 11" grid. Here's your second puzzle rated as difficult.

	4					6		1
				2	9			
6					1	2		
2		5			7		8	6
1	7		3			4		5
		6	9					8
			5	3				
5		9					7	

Sudoku puzzles © Wayne Gould

Even though they are both rated as difficult, and they both have 26 numbers identified, this puzzle is more challenging than the first.

Step 1:

As before, to quickly fill in the grid I begin by looking for pairs along horizontal lines in rows 1-3, then 4-6 and finally 7-9. To add order to this method I begin with the lowest numbers and work my way up to the highest numbers.

Working by rows I see that I can add the following:
'2' in R1C3
'6' in R2C4

	4	2				6		1
			6	2	9			
6					1	2		
2		5			7		8	6
1	7		3			4		5
		6	9					8
			5	3				
5		9					7	

It looks like that's all we'll be able to add by rows.

Step 2:

Now I am looking for pairs along vertical lines in columns 1-3, then 4-6 and finally 7-9. As before, to add order to this method I begin with the lowest numbers and work my way up to the highest numbers.

Working by columns I see that I can add the following:
'6' in R5C2
'3' in R1C6
'8' in R2C7
'6' in R8C8

	4	2			3	6		1
			6	2	9	8		
6					1	2		
2		5			7		8	6
	6							
1	7		3			4		5
		6	9					8
			5	3			6	
5		9					7	

Not bad, we've added six numbers to the grid fairly quickly.

Step 3:

Now I look for Alleys. Again, these are Boxes that have 3 open spaces in a single Box along either the horizontal or vertical with most of the other numbers filled in that Box.

	4	2			3	6		1
			6	2	9	8		
6					1	2		
2		5			7		8	6
	6							
1	7		3			4		5
		6	9					8
			5	3			6	
5		9					7	

Look in Box 8. We have an Alley in the 9th row. By using the 7 in the Alley and the '7' in R4C6 we know we can place a '7' in R7C5. Go ahead and plug in '7' in R7C5.

While we have a number of other Alleys none of them eliminate all the possibilities for an individual square.

Step 4:

Now I look for rows, columns and Boxes where I can easily spot most or all of the numbers 1-9.

	4	2			3	6		1
			6	2	9	8		
6					1	2		
2		5			7		8	6
	6							
1	7		3			4		5
		6	9	7				8
			5	3			6	
5		9					7	

Look at R6C3. I see all the numbers '1' through '9' except '8'.

Go ahead and plug '8' into R6C3.

Many of the other Boxes, rows and columns come close but don't totally eliminate all but one number.

Step 5:

Now I want to start identifying possibilities. I look for rows, columns and Boxes where most of the numbers are already filled in.

At this point we'll limit our work to Boxes, rows & columns that have 3 or 4 open squares. Then we'll move on to step 6 before going back to completely fill in all the possibilities.

789	4	2	78	58	3	6	59	1
		137	6	2	9	8		
6		37	478	458	1	2		
2	39	5	14	149	7	139	8	6
349	6	34						
1	7	8	3	69	26	4	29	5
		6	9	7				8
		147	5	3			6	
5		9					7	

Go ahead and fill in the possibilities for Boxes, rows & columns that have 3 or 4 open squares. Did you get the same possibilities listed above? Let's see if we can find any solutions with our new information.

Look at Box 3. We must have a '5' in the 8th column of Box 3, because we can't have it in the 9th column due to the '5' in R6C9 and the 7th column is already full in Box 3.

789	4	2	78	58	3	6	59	1
		137	6	2	9	8		
6		37	478	458	1	2		
2	39	5	14	149	7	139	8	6
349	6	34						
1	7	8	3	69	26	4	29	5
		6	9	7		5		8
		147	5	3			6	
5		9					7	

Because we know we'll have a '5' in Box 3, C8 we can't have a '5' in C8 of Box 9. So the '5' must go in C7 of Box 9 where two of the rows are already filled with 5's so that leaves only R7C7 for the '5'.

Let's plug that '5' in R7C7.

We now have another row, R7, and another column C7 with only 4 open squares. Let's fill in the possibilities.

789	4	2	78	58	3	6	59	1
		137	6	2	9	8		
6		37	478	458	1	2		
2	39	5	14	149	7	139	8	6
349	6	34			5	7		
1	7	8	3	69	26	4	29	5
34	123	6	9	7	24	5	1234	8
		147	5	3		19	6	
5		9				13	7	

Look at Box 2. The '5' for Box 2 must be in C5 because C4 in Box 2 has no 5's and C6 in Box 2 is already filled. Because of that the '5' for Box 5 can't be in C5. Because we've got a '5 in R8C4 and in R6C9 there is only one open square in Box 5 for a '5' at R5C6.

Look at C7. We need a '7' in that column. The '7' can't be in C7 of Box 9 because we already have a '7' in that Box. It can't be in R4 because we already have a '7' there. The '7' must go in R5C7. You can confirm this by examining the possibilities. There's only one '7' in the possibilities for C7.

Remember to eliminate possibilities after plugging in the '5' in R5C6 and the '7' in R5C7.

789	4	<u>2</u>	78	58	3	6	59	1
		137	<u>6</u>	2	9	<u>8</u>		
6		37	478	458	1	2		
2	39	5	14	149	7	139	8	6
349	<u>6</u>	34		<u>5</u>	~~3~~<u>7</u>~~9~~			
1	7	<u>8</u>	3	69	26	4	29	5
34	123	6	9	<u>7</u>	24	<u>5</u>	1234	8
		147	5	3	248	19	<u>6</u>	
5		9			2468	13	7	

The addition of new numbers gives us C6 with only 4 open squares. Let's fill in those possibilities.

Before identifying ALL the possibilities I like to go through steps 1 through 5 quickly to see if I can identify any other numbers.

A single number can be the difference between solving a puzzle quickly and spending a lot of extra time and effort trying to figure it out.

Unfortunately at this point I don't see any other opportunities to eliminate numbers so we'll have to go through the process of identifying all the possibilities.

This isn't as difficult as it may seem at first. With practice you can quickly identify the possibilities.

789	4	2	78	58	3	6	59	1
37	135	137	6	2	9	8	345	347
6	3589	37	478	458	1	2	3459	3479
2	39	5	14	149	7	139	8	6
349	6	34	1248	1489	5	79	1239	239
1	7	8	3	69	26	4	29	5
34	123	6	9	7	24	5	1234	8
478	128	147	5	3	248	19	6	249
5	1238	9	1248	1468	2468	13	7	234

Here are all the possibilities. Your puzzle should look exactly like the one above.

Step 6:

It is time to look for 4 different occurrences.
   a) Numbers that only occur once in a Box, row or column.
   b) Twins that eliminate possibilities.
   c) Triplets that eliminate possibilities.
   d) Quads that eliminate possibilities

Look at Box 1. There's a triplet, 137, in the three squares R2C1, R2C3 and R3C3. Let's eliminate 137 from the other squares in Box 1.

789	4	2	78	58	3	6	59	1
37	5	137	6	2	9	8	345	347
6	3589	37	478	458	1	2	3459	3479
2	39	5	14	149	7	139	8	6
349	6	34	1248	1489	5	79	1239	239
1	7	8	3	69	26	4	29	5
34	123	6	9	7	24	5	1234	8
478	128	47	5	3	248	19	6	249
5	1238	9	1248	1468	2468	13	7	234

Good news. We've eliminated all the possibilities for R2C2 except '5'. Let's plug that in and eliminate '5' as a possibility in Box 1, R2 and C2.

There's more good news. R2 now has only one '1' and
that's in R2C3. Let's plug that in and eliminate
possibilities.

R1 also has only one '7' and that's in R1C4. Let's plug
that in and eliminate possibilities.

~~7~~89	**4**	<u>2</u>	**7**~~8~~	58	**3**	**6**	59	**1**
37	<u>~~3~~</u>**5**	<u>1</u>~~37~~	<u>6</u>	**2**	**9**	<u>8</u>	34~~5~~	347
6	~~3~~589	37	4~~7~~8	458	**1**	**2**	3459	3479
2	39	**5**	14	149	**7**	139	**8**	**6**
349	**6**	34	1248	1489	**5**	~~39~~**7**~~9~~	1239	239
1	**7**	<u>8</u>	**3**	69	26	**4**	29	**5**
34	123	**6**	**9**	<u>7</u>	24	**5**	1234	**8**
478	128	~~4~~47	**5**	**3**	248	19	<u>6</u>	249
5	1238	**9**	1248	1468	2468	13	**7**	234

That one twin helped us fill in three squares.

Unfortunately, I don't see any more twins, triplets or quads
that help us eliminate possibilities.

Before we move on to step seven, I'd like to mention that at this point in solving difficult puzzles we will typically work through several clues until we find the one solution for a square that unlocks the puzzle and allows us to fill in all the other squares using our previously discussed steps.

A properly conceived Sudoku puzzle should NOT require guessing. There should always be a clue.

Some puzzles have more than one solution. In other words, at some point you have to guess. I consider these types of puzzles to be defective. Sudoku is a game of logic, not guessing.

Two different people may solve a puzzle differently as far as order of found numbers is concerned but a properly conceived puzzle will always result in the same final solution.

So, if you find a clue in Step 7 but haven't unlocked the puzzle then you need to continue searching for clues. They are there. You may need to find 3 or more clues before you unlock a difficult puzzle.

It's time to move on to Step 7. Put on your thinking cap.

Step 7:

It is time to analyze situations where a set of numbers eliminates another number based upon the position of those numbers on the grid. This is the part that requires the most thinking.

≠89 **4**	**2**	7̵8 ₅₈	**3**	**6** ₅₉	**1**
₃₇ ±5	1̵3̵7̵	**6**	**2**	**9**	**8** ₃₄₅ ₃₄₇
6 ₃̵5̵89 ₃₇	4̵8 ₄₅₈	**1**	**2** ₃̵59 ₃̵79
2 ₃₉	**5** ₁₄ ₁₄₉	**7** ₁₃₉	**8**	**6**
₃₄₉ **6** ₃₄	12̵8 1̵89	**5** ±7̵9 ₁₂₃₉	₂₃₉
1	**7**	**8**	**3** ₆₉ ₂₆	**4** ₂₉	**5**
₃₄ ₁₂₃	**6**	**9**	**7** ₂₄	**5** ₁₂₃₄	**8**
₄₇₈ ₁₂₈ ±47	**5**	**3** ₂₄₈	₁₉ **6**	₂₄₉
5 ₁₂₃₈	**9** ₁₂₄₈ ₁₄₆₈ ₂₄₆₈	₁₃ **7** ₂₃₄

Look at Box 3. All the 4's for R2 fall in Box 3. That means there can't be 4's in any other squares in Box 3 besides R2. We can eliminate the 4's in R3C8 and R3C9.

Look at Box 5. All the 4's for R4 fall in Box 5. That means there can't be 4's in any other squares in Box 5 besides R4. We can eliminate the 4's in R5C4 and R5C5.

Look at Box 8. All the 4's and 8's for C6 fall in Box 8. That means there can't be 4's or 8's in any other squares in Box 8 besides C6. We can eliminate the 4's & 8's in R9C4 and R9C5.

≠89 **4**	**2**	**7₈** 58	**3**	**6** 59	**1**
37 ≠3**5**	**1**₃₇	**6** 2	**9**	**8** 34≠5	347
6 ₃≠89 37	4≠8 458	**1**	**2** 3≠59	3≠79	
2 39	**5** 14 149	**7** 139	**8**	**6**	
349 **6** 34	12≠8 1≠89	**5** ≠3**7**₉ 1239	239		
1 **7** **8**	**3** 69 26	**4** 29	**5**		
34 123 **6**	**9** **7** 24	**5** 1234	**8**		
478 128 ≠47	**5** **3** 248	19 **6** 249			
5 ≠238 **9**	12≠8 1≠6₈ 2468	≠3 **7** 234			

Also in Box 8, all the 1's for Box 8 fall in R9C4 & R9C5. That means there can't be any other 1's in R9 besides those in Box 8. We can eliminate the 1's in R9C2 and R9C7. <u>When we do that we find the R9C7 is down to a single possibility.</u>

At last, that one number is what we've been looking for. Let's plug in the '3' in R9C7, eliminate possibilities and see if it unlocks the puzzle.

After plugging in the '3' in R9C7 and eliminating, it is time to review. I see that by eliminating the '3' in R4C7 we now have only one '3' in R4 and that is in square R4C2. Let's plug that in, eliminate possibilities and see where it takes us.

₹89	4	2	7₈	58	3	6	59	1
37	₊₃5	1₃₇	6	2	9	8	345	347
6	₉₅89	37	4₹8	458	1	2	3₊59	3₹79
2	3₉	5	14	149	7	1₃9	8	6
₃₊9	6	₃4	12₊8	1₊89	5	₊₃7₉	1239	239
1	7	8	3	69	26	4	29	5
34	12₉	6	9	7	24	5	12₃4	8
478	128	₊₊7	5	3	248	19	6	249
5	₊2₃8	9	12₊8	1₊68	2468	₊3	7	2₃4

By plugging '3' into R4C2 we find that R5C3 has only one possibility left, a '4'. Let's plug that in, eliminate possibilities.

That gave us two squares with only one possibility. The square R5C1 in Box 4 has only the '9' remaining and the square R8C3 in Box 7 has only the '7' remaining as possibilities.

Let's start at the top by plugging in the '9' in R5C1.

8	4	2	7 8	5 8	3	6	5 9	1
3 7	5	1 37	6	2	9	8	3 4 5	3 4 7
6	3 5 8 9	3 7	4 7 8	4 5 8	1	2	3 4 5 9	3 4 7 9
2	3 9	5	1 4	1 4 9	7	1 9 9	8	6
9	6	4	1 2 4 8	1 4 8 9	5	7	1 2 3 9	2 3 9
1	7	8	3	6 9	2 6	4	2 9	5
3 4	1 2 9	6	9	7	2 4	5	1 2 9 4	8
4 7 8	1 2 8	7	5	3	2 4 8	1 9	6	2 4 9
5	2 9 8	9	1 2 4 8	1 4 6 8	2 4 6 8	3	7	2 9 4

By plugging in the '9' in R5C1 and eliminating we see that R1C1 has only one possibility '8'. Before we plug in R8C3, let's work from the top down and plug in R1C1 with the '8'.

Doing that reveals two more squares with only one possibility, R3C2 has only the '9' left and R1C5 has only the '5' remaining. We now have three squares with only one possibility.

It looks like we've unlocked this puzzle. We'll see.

Let's work through it by starting at the top and plugging in the '5' in R1C5.

Plugging in the '5' in R1C5 and eliminating provides us
with the solution to R1C8, the '9'. Let's plug that in.
Don't forget that we still have two more squares with only
one number remaining in R3C2 and R8C3.

₇**8**₉	4	2	**7**₈	**5**₈	3	6	₅**9**	1
₃₇	₁₃**5**	**1**₃₇	**6**	2	9	**8**	₃₄₅	₃₄₇
6	₃₅₈₉	₃₇	₄₇₈	₄₅₈	1	2	₃₄₅₉	₃₄₇₉
2	**3**₉	5	₁₄	₁₄₉	7	₁₃₉	8	6
₃₄**9**	**6**	₃**4**	₁₂₄₈	₁₄₈₉	5	₁₃**7**₉	₁₂₃₉	₂₃₉
1	7	**8**	3	₆₉	₂₆	4	₂₉	5
₃₄	₁₂₉	6	9	**7**	₂₄	**5**	₁₂₉₄	8
₄₇₈	₁₂₈	₄₄₇	5	3	₂₄₈	₁₉	**6**	₂₄₉
5	₄₂₉₈	9	₁₂₄₈	₁₄₆₈	₂₄₆₈	₄**3**	7	₂₉₄

Plugging in the '9' in R1C8 and eliminating leaves us with
only one possibility in R6C8, the '2'. Before we plug that
in I'd like you to notice that C8 has only one '5' and it is in
R3C8. Since R3C8 has to be a '5' we can eliminate the '3'
as a possibility in R3C8.

Working from the top, let's plug in the '9' in R3C2.

Plugging in the '9' in R3C2 doesn't reveal any additional solutions. Let's plug the '5' in R3C8 and eliminate possibilities.

7 8 9	4	2	7 8	5 8	3	6	5 9	1
3 7	5	1 9 7	6	2	9	8	3 4 5	3 4 7
6	9 5 8 9	3 7	4 7 8	4 5 8	1	2	3 4 5 9	3 4 7 9
2	3 9	5	1 4	1 4 9	7	1 3 9	8	6
3 4 9	6	3 4	1 2 4 8	1 4 8 9	5	1 3 7 9	1 2 3 9	2 3 9
1	7	8	3	6 9	2 6	4	2 9	5
3 4	1 2 9	6	9	7	2 4	5	1 2 3 4	8
4 7 8	1 2 8	4 4 7	5	3	2 4 8	1 9	6	2 4 9
5	2 3 8	9	1 2 4 8	1 4 6 8	2 4 6 8	3	7	2 3 4

Plugging the '5' in R3C8 doesn't reveal any additional solutions. Let's plug the '2' in R6C8 and eliminate.

Plugging in the '2' in R6C8 provides us with two new squares that have only one solution remaining, R5C9 and R6C6.

Let's plug a '3' in R5C9 since it is the topmost known square.

Plugging in the '3' in R5C9 provides us with two new squares that have only one solution remaining, R3C9 and R5C8. Let's plug the '7' in R3C9 and eliminate.

₇8₉	4	2	7₈	5₈	3	6	₅9	1
3 7	₄₉5	1₃₇	6	2	9	8	3 4 5	₃4₇
6	₃₅₈9	3 7	4 7 8	4 5 8	1	2	₃₄5₉	₃₄7₉
2	3₉	5	1 4	1 4 9	7	1 ₃ 9	8	6
₃₄9	6	₃4	1 2 ₄ 8	1 ₄ 8 9	5	₄₉7₉	1 ₂ ₃ 9	₈3₉
1	7	8	3	6 9	₂6	4	2₉	5
3 4	1 2 ₉	6	9	7	2 4	5	1 ₂ ₃ 4	8
4 7 8	1 2 8	₄₇7	5	3	2 4 8	1 9	6	2 ₄ 9
5	₄2₉8	9	1 2 ₄ 8	1 ₄ 6 8	2 4 6 8	₄3	7	2 ₃ ₄

Plugging in the '7' in R3C9 provides us with two new squares that have only one solution remaining, R2C9 and R3C3. Let's plug the '4' in R2C9 and eliminate.

Plugging in the '4' in R2C9 provides us with two new squares that have only one solution remaining, R2C8 and R9C9. Let's plug the '3' in R2C8 and eliminate.

At this point I'm confident we've unlocked the puzzle. Let's work through it.

Plugging in the '3' in R2C8 provides us with one new square that has only one solution remaining, R2C1. Let's plug the '7' in R2C1 and eliminate.

₇<u>8</u>₉	4	<u>2</u>	<u>7</u>₈	<u>5</u>₈	<u>3</u>	6	₅<u>9</u>	1
₉<u>7</u>	₄₆<u>5</u>	<u>1</u>₃₇	<u>6</u>	2	9	8	<u>3</u>₄₅	₉<u>4</u>₇
6	₃₅₈<u>9</u>	<u>3</u>₇	₄₇8	₄₅8	1	2	₃₄<u>5</u>₉	₃₄<u>7</u>₉
2	<u>3</u>₉	5	₁₄	₁₄₉	7	₁₃₉	8	6
₃₄<u>9</u>	<u>6</u>	₃<u>4</u>	₁₂₄8	₁₄8₉	<u>5</u>	₁₃<u>7</u>₉	₁₃₉₉	₉<u>3</u>₉
1	7	<u>8</u>	3	₆₉	₂6	4	<u>2</u>₉	5
₃₄	₁₂₉	6	9	<u>7</u>	₂₄	<u>5</u>	₁₃₄	8
₄₇8	₁₂8	₄₄7	5	3	₂₄8	₁₉	<u>6</u>	₂₄₉
5	₂₉8	9	₁₂₄8	₁₄₆8	₂₄₆8	₄<u>3</u>	7	₂₉₄

Plugging in the '7' in R2C1 reveals another square with only one solution, R8C1. Right now we have six squares that have only one solution R3C3, R5C8, R6C6, R8C1, R8C3 and R9C9. Let's work from the top down and plug the '3' in R3C3.

Plugging the '3' in R3C3 did not reveal any new solutions for the unsolved squares.

At this point we have most of the puzzle solved so we can proceed through the rest very quickly.

Let's plug in the '1' in R5C8 and the '8' in R5C5.

Plugging the '1' in R5C8 provides the solution for three more squares, R4C7, R5C5 and R7C8.

Plugging the '8' in R5C5 reveals the solution for two more squares, R3C5 and R5C4.

₇8₉	4	2	7₈	5₈	3	6	₅9	1
₉7	₊₃5	1₉₇	6	2	9	8	3₄₅	₉4₇
6	₃₅₉9	3₇	4₇8	4₅8	1	2	₃₄5₉	₃₄7₉
2	3₉	5	14	149	7	₊₉9	8	6
₉₊9	6	₉4	₊2₊8	₊₊8₉	5	₊₃7₉	1₂₃₉	₂3₉
1	7	8	3	69	₂6	4	2₉	5
34	12₉	6	9	7	24	5	₊₂₉4	8
4₇8	128	₊₄7	5	3	248	19	6	2₊9
5	₊2₉8	9	12₊8	1₊68	2468	₊3	7	2₉₊

Have you ever come across a puzzle where you only had a few squares left but still couldn't solve the puzzle. Chances are you missed something. While it is tempting to forge ahead and fill in all the known squares without eliminating it could cause problems.

Be sure to eliminate possibilities as you continue to plug in new numbers.

Right now we have eight squares that have only one solution R3C5, R4C7, R5C4, R6C6, R7C8, R8C1, R8C3 and R9C9. Let's continue with our process filling in these eight known squares and eliminating. Rather than walk you through each of these one-by-one go ahead and fill them in and eliminate on your own.

Does your puzzle match the one below?

₇8₉	4	2	7₈	5₈	3	6	₅9	1
₉7	₃₆5	1₃₇	6	2	9	8	3₄₅	₉4₇
6	₃₅₈9	3₇	₄₇8	4₅₈	1	2	₃₄5₉	₃₄7₉
2	3₉	5	14	1₄₉	7	₃9	8	6
₃₄9	6	₃4	₁2₄₈	₁₄8₉	5	₁₃7₉	1₂₃₉	₂3₉
1	7	8	3	₆9	₂6	4	2₉	5
3₄	12₃	6	9	7	2₄	5	₁₂₃4	8
4₇₈	128	₁₄7	5	3	2₄8	1₉	6	₂₄9
5	₁₂₃8	9	1₂₄8	1₄68	₂468	₄3	7	2₃₄

Plugging in those eight numbers provided us with solutions for nine more squares: R3C4, R4C5, R6C5, R7C1, R7C6, R8C7, R8C9, R9C2, and R9C4.

We're almost finished. Let's continue with our process filling in these nine known squares and eliminating.

Go ahead and fill in the nine squares: R3C4, R4C5, R6C5, R7C1, R7C6, R8C7, R8C9, R9C2 and R9C4. To make it easier to see, I'll erase the old underlining and start with these nine squares.

Does your puzzle match the one below?

8	4	2	7	5	3	6	9	1
7	5	1	6	2	9	8	3	4
6	9	3	8	4	1	2	5	7
2	3	5	4	1	7	9	8	6
9	6	4	2	8	5	7	1	3
1	7	8	3	9	6	4	2	5
3		6	9	7	2	5	4	8
4		7	5	3		1	6	9
5	8	9	1			3	7	2

Plugging in those nine numbers provide us with the solutions for the last six squares: R4C4, R7C2, R8C2, R8C6, R9C5 and R9C6.

Go ahead and plug those numbers into the puzzle.

Congratulations you did it!

Here's the finished puzzle.

8	4	2	7	5	3	6	9	1
7	5	1	6	2	9	8	3	4
6	9	3	8	4	1	2	5	7
2	3	5	4	1	7	9	8	6
9	6	4	2	8	5	7	1	3
1	7	8	3	9	6	4	2	5
3	1	6	9	7	2	5	4	8
4	2	7	5	3	8	1	6	9
5	8	9	1	6	4	3	7	2

Whenever I finish a puzzle I like to take a moment to glance over the Boxes, rows & columns to make certain I don't have duplicate numbers.

Summary

Step 1: To quickly fill in the grid begin by looking for pairs along horizontal lines in rows 1-3, then 4-6 and finally 7-9. To add order to this method, begin with the lowest numbers and work up to the highest numbers.

Step 2: Look for pairs along vertical lines in columns 1-3, then 4-6 and finally 7-9. Begin with the lowest numbers and work up to the highest numbers.

Step 3: Look for 'Alleys'. These are Boxes that have 3 open spaces in a single Box along either the horizontal or vertical with most of the other numbers filled in that Box.

Step 4: Look for rows, columns and Boxes where you can easily spot most or all of the numbers 1-9. From this point forward begin repeating previous steps for each new number you are able to plug in.

Step 5: Start identifying possibilities. Look for rows, columns and Boxes where most of the numbers are already filled in.

Step 6: Look for 4 different occurrences.
1. Numbers that only occur once in a Box, row or column.
2. Twins that eliminate possibilities.
3. Triplets that eliminate possibilities.
4. Quads that eliminate possibilities

Step 7: Analyze situations where a set of numbers eliminates another number based upon the position of those numbers on the grid.

Glossary

Alley – a group of 3 open squares in a box, along either a vertical or horizontal line, where most of the other numbers in the box a known.

Box – a 3x3 group of squares that form a square. There are nine boxes in a Sudoku puzzle, numbered 1 through 9 starting in the upper left, moving left to right, then top to bottom and finishing in the lower right.

Column – a group of 9 squares along a vertical line.

Elimination – the process of narrowing the possible numbers that can be plugged into a square.

Quad - whenever there are only four possibilities for four squares in a Box, row or column.

Possibilities – the numbers that could be plugged into in any given square.

R1C1 – shorthand for the 1st Row, 1st Column, and any number 2 through 9 may be substituted for the number '1'.

Row – a group of 9 squares along a horizontal line.

Square – the place where you write a number.

Twin – whenever there are only two possibilities for two squares in a Box, row or column.

Triplet - whenever there are only three possibilities for three squares in a Box, row or column.

A Final Thought

I'd like to revisit the point I made earlier about guessing.

I don't like spending 15 minutes working through a difficult puzzle only to find out that it is a guessing game instead of a logic game. A properly conceived Sudoku puzzle should NOT require guessing. There should always be a clue. I consider Sudoku puzzles that require guessing to be defective.

If a puzzle has more than one solution then at some point you'll have to guess. Think about it. If there are two different solutions then it means that at some point you could put two different numbers in the same square. That means you couldn't or didn't eliminate all other possibilities. Which can only mean it was a guess.

There is another instance where you might have to guess and yet there would be only one solution. In those cases you haven't been given enough information. Think about it. I could give you a puzzle with only a few numbers filled in. Not enough clues mean you'd have to guess. The chances are good that there would be more than one solution in that extreme example. Nevertheless, you get the idea. If you weren't provided enough information you would have to guess.

With today's computing power we should never have defective puzzles. Sudoku can be extremely fun and challenging without guessing.

Have a good time!

Blank

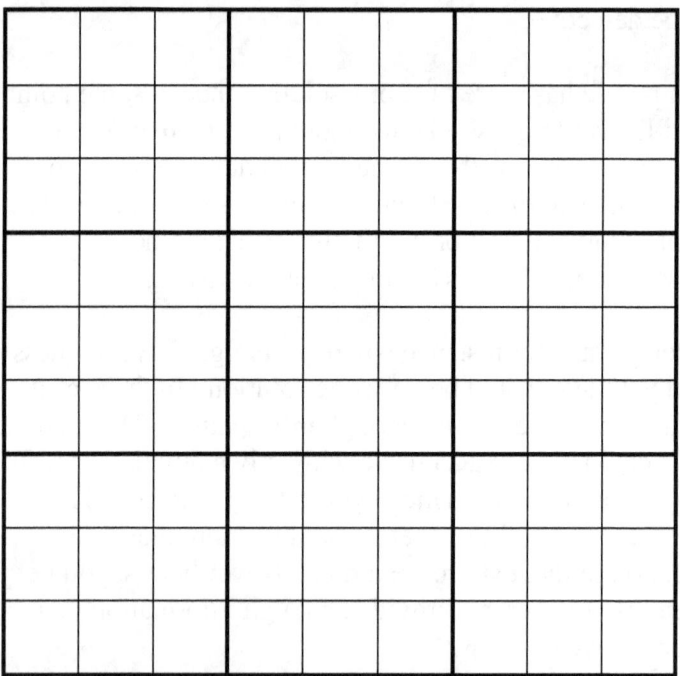

www.ingramcontent.com/pod-product-compliance
Lightning Source LLC
Chambersburg PA
CBHW071252170526
45165CB00003B/1306